Tom and Ricky

and the

Falling Star Mystery

Bob Wright

D0778257

High Noon Books
Novato, California

Cover Design: Nancy Peach
Interior Illustrations: Herb Heidinger

Glossary: clothes, flashlight, high, meteor, space, dollars, museum hundreds, metal, secret, satellite

International Standard Book Number: 0-87879-341-0

8 7 6 5 4 3 2 1 0 9
5 4 3 2 1 0 9 8 7 6

High Noon Books
a division of ATP
20 Commercial Blvd.
Novato, California 94949

Contents

CHAPTER 1

The Meteor

Ricky was about to go to sleep. He looked out at the stars in the sky. The night sky was dark and clear.

All at once, he saw something bright moving fast in the sky. Patches saw it, too. He barked.

"What was that?" Ricky said to his dog.

Ricky jumped out of bed. It looked like a star was falling from the sky.

"It landed in the field over there," Ricky said. "A falling star has landed!"

Ricky put his clothes on. He also put on a warm coat. Then he got a flashlight. He started for the door.

"Ricky, I thought you were in bed. Where are you going?" his mother said.

"I saw a falling star. It came down near here. I am going to look for it," Ricky said.

"Now? But it's late and it's dark," Ricky's mother said.

"I'll be careful," Ricky answered.

"You stay right here. You can look for it in the morning," his mother said.

"Oh, Mom," Ricky said. He went back to bed. But he couldn't stop thinking about the falling star.

Ricky went to see Tom the next morning. He told his friend about the falling star.

"Just what is a falling star?" Tom asked.

"A falling star is a *meteor*. That's a rock that falls from space," Ricky said.

"A rock? But you told me it lit up the sky. How can a rock do that?" Tom asked.

"The meteor gets very hot as it falls. It gets hot because it is falling so fast. The air makes the meteor very bright," Ricky said.

"Where did the meteor fall?" Tom asked.

"In the big field," Ricky answered.

"Come on! Let's look for it," Tom said.

Patches barked. "You can come, too. You can help us look," Ricky said.

Tom and Ricky rode their bikes to the field. They locked the bikes. Then they started to look for the meteor.

"This will not be easy. The grass is high. And this is a big field," Tom said.

"You start over there. I'll look on this side of the field," Ricky said.

"I'm not sure what I'm looking for. What does a meteor look like?" Tom said.

"It looks like a rock. But it will be all black and burned. Remember, the meteor got very hot as it fell," Ricky answered.

Tom and Ricky started to look. Patches was running around. He wanted to help. He thought the boys were playing some new game.

4

They looked and looked. But all they found was junk. And all kinds of rocks. But no meteor.

Then Tom called, "Ricky! Come over here. I have found something!"

"Is it the meteor?" Ricky asked.

"No. I don't know what it is. I have never seen anything like it," Tom answered.

CHAPTER 2

The Metal Ball

Ricky ran to his friend. Tom was holding a metal ball. The ball was all burned and black.

"Maybe this is what you saw fall from the sky," Tom said. He gave the ball to Ricky.

Ricky looked at the metal ball. He turned it over in his hands. The ball seemed to be made of two parts.

Patches was jumping up and down. He wanted to look, too.

"What do you think it is?" Tom asked.

Ricky looked closely at the metal ball. "This is no meteor. A meteor is a rock from space," he said.

"Then what is it?" Tom asked again.

"It's just some junk. The field is full of junk like this." Ricky said. He started to throw the ball to the ground.

"Wait a minute. Let me take another look at it," Tom said.

Ricky handed the metal ball to his friend. Tom turned the top of the ball. He opened it. The ball opened into two parts.

There was a small metal can in it. The can fell to the ground. Patches picked it up and ran off with it.

"Come back with that!" Ricky yelled.

But Patches liked the game. He would not come back with the can.

Patches picked it up and ran off with it.

Tom laughed. "Patches is going to hide the can. He thinks this is a game."

But Ricky did not laugh.

"Patches could get hurt. There is an old well on that side of the field. Patches could fall in."

The grass in the field was high. The boys could not see where Patches had gone. They both yelled for the dog to come back. Where could that dog have gone?

All of a sudden, Patches came back. He was wagging his tail. But Ricky was mad. "You could have fallen in the well," he said.

They looked for the meteor some more. But they couldn't find it. All they found was more junk.

"Maybe we should give up looking for that meteor," Tom said.

"Do you have something better to do?" Ricky asked his friend.

"Yes. How would you like to make some money?" Tom answered.

"How?" Ricky asked.

Tom picked up the metal ball they had found. "We could sell this. Mr. Wood owns a junk yard near here. He buys old junk like this," he said.

"Do you think he would buy that thing?" Ricky asked.

"Sure. He buys all kinds of things," Tom said.

"Let's go to see him. Let's see what he says," Ricky said.

"Come on. I could use the money," Tom said.

"OK. Let's go! I can always use some money, too," Ricky said.

CHAPTER 3

At the Junk Yard

Ricky and Tom got on their bikes. They rode over to Mr. Wood's junk yard.

"Hello, Mr. Wood," Tom said.

"Hello, Tom. What can I do for you today?" Mr. Wood asked.

"Would you like to buy some junk?" Tom asked. He showed Mr. Wood the metal ball.

"What is it?" Mr. Wood asked.

"I don't know. Ricky and I found it in the big field near here," Tom answered.

Mr. Wood looked at the metal ball. He was not sure he wanted to buy it.

"It's good junk," Tom said.

"Good for what? I'm not sure that it is worth much. Who would want to buy something like this?" Mr. Wood asked.

"Oh, come on. Someone will want to buy it," Ricky said.

Mr. Wood picked up the metal ball. He didn't say anything. He just looked at it. Then he said, "OK. I'll give you five dollars for it."

"Sold!" said Tom.

Mr. Wood gave the boys the money.

"Thanks a lot, Mr. Wood. See you later!" Ricky said.

Ricky and Tom rode home on their bikes. The boys were happy they had made some money. But Ricky was thinking.

"We could make a lot more money," Ricky said to his friend.

"Right! Let's go back to the field. There is lots of junk there. We can sell it to Mr. Wood," Tom said.

"No. We can't make very much money just selling junk. All we got for that metal ball was five dollars," Ricky answered.

"It's more than we had before," Tom said.

"Yes, but I know how we can make a lot more money," Ricky answered.

"How?" Tom asked.

"We could make a lot of money if we found that meteor," Ricky said.

Tom laughed. "Who would pay money for a rock from space?" he asked.

"A museum," Ricky answered.

"A museum?" Tom asked.

"Yes, a museum," Ricky answered.

"Why?" Tom asked.

"The people at museums look at meteors," Ricky said.

"Why is that?" Tom asked.

"Meteors help them to know more about space," Ricky said.

"How much would a museum pay us for that meteor?" Tom asked.

"Maybe hundreds of dollars," Ricky said.

"Hundreds of dollars! So what are we waiting for? Come on! Let's go look for that meteor," Tom said.

"Right! But let's leave Patches home this time. I don't want him to fall into that old well," Ricky answered.

"Let's get going," Tom said.

Ricky put Patches inside the house. Then the two boys got on their bikes. They started to ride back to the big field.

"I sure hope that we find the meteor this time," Tom said.

"We will keep looking until we do. And then we will sell it!" Ricky answered.

"We made some money on that metal ball," Tom said.

"We should get much more for the meteor," Ricky said.

"You bet we will," Tom said.

They went as fast as they could back to the big field.

CHAPTER 4

The Man in the Field

Ricky and Tom walked back into the field. They wanted to find that meteor.

But this time they were not alone. There was a man in the field. He was looking for something. The man was holding a long pole with a metal pan on the end.

"Who is that? And what is he holding?" Tom asked.

"That long pole helps him find metal," Ricky answered.

The man looked up. "What are you doing here?" he said to the boys. He looked mean.

Tom and Ricky looked at him.

"What are you doing here?" he said to the boys. He looked mean.

"I saw a falling star last night. We think it landed here. Are you looking for it, too?" Ricky answered.

The man got mad. "No. I'm not looking for a falling star. I'm just looking for . . . junk," he answered.

"You can't sell junk for a lot of money. You can sell a meteor for a lot of money," Tom said.

"Would you help us look for it? Meteors have metal in them. Maybe we could find it with your long pole," Ricky asked.

"Then we could sell the meteor," Tom said.

Ricky hoped that the man would help them. He tried to be friendly. "I'm Ricky. This is my friend Tom. What's your name?"

"Bert," the man answered.

"So how about it, Bert? Will you help us?" Ricky asked.

"No. I told you that I'm looking for junk. You will never find that meteor," Bert said.

"Why not?" Tom asked.

"Meteors almost always burn up in the air. Very few get to the ground," Bert answered.

"Maybe this one did," Ricky said.

"Then I would have found it. This pole helps me find metal. And meteors are mostly made of metal," Bert said.

"Maybe he is right. Let's give up. We already have five dollars from the junk we sold. So let's go spend it," Tom said.

Ricky wasn't sure. But he didn't like the way Bert was looking at them.

"OK. Let's go," Ricky said to Tom.

They left the field.

Bert was happy to see the boys go. Then he thought of something. "Wait. Where did you find that junk you sold?" he asked.

"Right here. We found an old metal ball. We sold it for five dollars," Tom answered.

"Where did you sell it?" Bert asked.

"At Mr. Wood's junk yard," Ricky said.

Bert waited for Tom and Ricky to leave. Then he left, too. He seemed to be in a big hurry.

"What's he doing?" Tom asked.

"He's sure in a hurry," Ricky said.

"Do you think he wants to buy that metal ball?" Tom asked.

"He might want it," Ricky said.

"But why would he want that thing?" Tom asked.

"I don't know. It sure seems funny, doesn't it?" Ricky said.

"It sure does," Tom said.

CHAPTER 5

Eddie Helps Out

"Let's go over to The Game Store. I want to play some video games. And we have five dollars to spend," Tom said to Ricky.

"OK. I guess Bert is right. The meteor must have burned up in the air," Ricky said.

The boys rode their bikes to The Game Store. They went in.

"Look, there's Eddie," Tom said.

"Hi, Tom. Hi, Ricky. What are you doing?" Eddie said to his friends.

"We made some money selling junk. So we have some to spend," Ricky said to Eddie.

"There is a new game here called *Meteor*. It's a lot of fun. Do you want to play it?" Eddie asked.

"*Meteor*? That's funny. We made our money looking for a real meteor," said Tom.

"What do you mean?" Eddie asked.

"I'll tell you. I saw a falling star last night. Tom and I went looking for it. But all we found was some junk," Ricky answered.

Tom went on. "We sold the junk for five dollars. We kept looking for the meteor. But we met a man. He told us that meteors burn up in the air."

"That isn't always so. Now and then meteors land on the earth," Eddie said.

"That's what I thought. But the man said they almost always burn up," Ricky said.

"Almost always. Tell me more about how the meteor looked," Eddie answered.

"It was a bright light in the sky. I saw it from my house," Ricky said.

"Did the light go out in the air?" Eddie asked his friend.

"No. I watched it all the way to the ground," Ricky answered.

"Then the meteor did land. You should have kept on looking for it. You could get a lot of money for a meteor," Eddie said.

"We looked for a long time. And Bert was looking, too. He had a way to find metal. That should have made it easy for him to find the meteor," Tom said.

"That pole that finds metal would be a big help. Why didn't Bert find it?" Eddie asked.

"Do you think the meteor is still in the field?" Ricky asked Eddie.

"It has to be there," Eddie answered.

Ricky looked at Tom.

"Thanks for your help. Come on, Tom. Let's go," Ricky said.

They ran for the door.

"Where are you going? I thought you wanted to play *Meteor*," Eddie yelled.

"We have to go," Tom said.

"What's this all about?" Eddie asked.

"We can't tell you all about it now," Ricky said.

"We're in a hurry. We have to go," Tom said.

"We are after a real meteor! We have to find it before Bert does," Ricky called out.

CHAPTER 6

The Hunt Goes On

The boys went to Ricky's house. Ricky put a rope on Patches.

"You can help us look for the meteor. But I don't want you to fall into that old well. This rope will keep you from running away," Ricky said to his dog.

Patches did not like the rope. But he was happy to be going out again. He wagged his tail and licked Ricky's face.

"Let's go!" said Tom.

Soon Ricky and Tom were back at the field.

"Where's Bert?" Tom asked.

"Maybe he gave up," Ricky answered.

"Or maybe he found the meteor. He had lots of time to look for it," Tom said.

"Let's look for it anyway. You start over there. Patches and I will look over here," Ricky said.

Just then they saw a car. A man got out. He began to walk over to the boys. It was Bert.

"I bet he didn't find the meteor. He came back to look for it again, too," Ricky said.

"Then where is his long pole?" Tom said. Bert did not have it with him.

"Now what's going on?" Ricky asked.

Bert came up to them. He looked mad.

"You have something I want," Bert said.

"What are you talking about?" Ricky asked.

"You found some junk," Bert said.

"We don't have it anymore. We sold it to Mr. Wood at the junk yard," Ricky answered.

"I know. I just came from the junk yard. I bought the metal ball from Mr. Wood. But something is missing," Bert said.

"What do you mean?" Tom asked.

"A metal can should have been inside the ball. What did you do with it?" Bert asked.

"We don't have the can. It fell out when we opened the ball. My dog ran off with it. Maybe he hid it somewhere," Ricky said.

"Make the dog bring it here," Bert said.

Then he pulled out a gun from his coat. "Do as I say!" he yelled.

Then he pulled out a gun from his coat. "Do as I say!" he yelled.

Ricky took the rope off Patches. "Go get the can you hid. Bring it here," he said to the dog.

Patches barked. But he would not go after the can. He did not want to leave Ricky. Patches didn't want Bert to hurt Ricky.

"I'll be all right, Patches. Go get the can," Ricky said.

Patches ran into the high grass. He knew that this was no game.

CHAPTER 7

Secrets from Space

All of a sudden, Patches came back. He had the metal can in his mouth. The dog dropped the can at Ricky's feet.

"Good dog," Ricky said.

Bert picked up the can. He looked at it. "This is it! This is what I have been looking for. It is going to make me a rich man," he said.

"But it's just junk," Tom said.

Bert laughed. "That's what you think!"

"What is in the can?" Ricky asked Bert.

"Secrets from space. That metal ball you found was a secret American space satellite. A lot of people have been looking for it," Bert

The dog dropped the can at Ricky's feet.

answered. He looked at Ricky.

"A satellite? I know a little about them," Ricky said.

"Do you mean one of those things they send up in rockets?" Tom asked.

"Yes. It had a small radio in it. The radio told me the satellite was coming down," Bert said.

"So it wasn't a meteor I saw. It was a falling satellite," Ricky said.

"Right. It got very hot falling in the sky. The satellite lit up the sky just like a meteor," Bert said.

"But why would a satellite come down in this field?" Ricky asked.

"It should have come down miles from here. That is where everyone is looking for it," Bert said.

"How did you know the satellite was here?" Ricky asked.

"I saw it fall just like you did. But I knew it was not a meteor. I knew that it was a secret satellite," Bert said.

"Then how come you didn't find it before we did?" Ricky asked.

"I had to buy that long pole. That took time. You got here before I did. And you found that metal ball, the satellite," Bert said.

"What are you going to do with the can?" Tom asked Bert.

"I'm going to sell it to some people. They will pay me well for American space secrets," Bert said.

Bert saw the rope on the ground. He knew what he had to do.

"I don't want you boys to go to the police. I need some time to get away from here. So I am going to tie you up," Bert said.

Bert put the can down and picked up the rope. He grabbed Tom. He began to tie him up with the rope.

Ricky started to run for help.

"Stop! Stop or I'll shoot!" Bert yelled.

CHAPTER 8

The Falling Spy

Bert tied Tom up with one end of the rope. Then he started to tie Ricky, too.

Patches didn't like what Bert was doing. He barked and barked.

"Shut up!" Bert yelled. But Patches kept barking. He wanted Bert to leave Ricky alone.

Then Patches tried something. He grabbed the metal can. Bert had left it on the ground.

"Drop that can!" Bert yelled.

But Patches ran off with it.

Bert ran after Patches. He could not see where the dog had gone. The grass was too high. "Bring that can back!" Bert yelled at Patches.

"Patches won't listen to what you say. He's my dog. He will only do what I say," Ricky said.

"OK. You tell him to bring me the can," Bert said.

"I have to find him first. Take this rope off so I can look for him," Ricky said.

"All right. We will all look for the dog," Bert said. He took the rope off Tom, too.

Ricky and Tom walked through the grass. Bert was behind them with his gun.

Patches came running over to Ricky. But he did not have the can with him.

"What did he do with the can?" Bert asked.

"He didn't have time to hide it. It must be around here somewhere," Tom said.

"I think I know where Patches dropped it. It's over there," Ricky said.

"Why did you tell him?" Tom asked.

"Stay where you are. I'll get it," Bert said. He ran to where Ricky said the can was.

All at once Bert yelled. The boys could not see him.

"Where is Bert?" Tom asked.

"He fell into the old well. That is where I wanted him to go," Ricky answered.

Just then they saw Sergeant Collins. He got out of his car. He ran over to Ricky and Tom.

"How did you know we needed help?" Tom

asked.

Tom and Ricky looked at Sergeant Collins.

All at once Bert yelled. The boys could not see him.

"Mr. Wood called the police. He heard about the satellite on TV. Then he knew what the metal ball was. He told us you had found it here. He told us about Bert, too," Sergeant Collins said.

Patches ran into the high grass. He came back with the metal can.

"The space secrets are safe!" Ricky said.

"Where is Bert?" Sergeant Collins asked.

"Bert fell into the old well," Tom said.

"The grass is high. Bert could not see the old well," Ricky said.

The policeman walked over to the well. Bert was down at the bottom. He was not hurt, but he was all wet.

Sergeant Collins looked at Ricky and Tom.

"You were looking for a falling star," he said.

"And you got a falling spy."